Book Two

BACH-SC  I

BASED ON EVENTS AND EPISODES OF BACH'S LIFE

The Purpose of the Bach-Schaum Edition

Johann Sebastian Bach (1685–1750) achieved almost legendary fame as a virtuoso performer in his own lifetime but has earned a unique position in musical history as the most inventive, creative, and important composer of the Baroque era. Many of his pieces were named Prelude, Sarabande, Minuet, Aria, Bourrée, or another term that refers to the form of the piece. This new Schaum edition presents a complete English suite, a complete French suite, and a complete Partita in an abridged arrangement. Other selections are given in their original form with some editorial fingering, phrasing, and pedaling. Explanatory notes, giving the student added appreciation of the greatness of Bach, precede each piece. This wealth of true biographical information adds musical appreciation to these authentic Bach excerpts.

Teachers will be happy to note that this Bach-Schaum book contains many examples of the musical forms for which Bach was famous.

Editor: Gail Lew
Production Coordinator: Karl Bork
Cover Illustration: Magdi Rodríguez
Cover Design: María A. Chenique

Contents

ENGLISH SUITE No. 3

A condensed arrangement of the complete suite

Bach wrote six "English Suites," each composed of six or more pieces. It is believed that Bach was familiar with the work of the English composer Henry Purcell and wrote these suites in the "English" style. Excerpts from all six pieces in the suite are presented here.

BWV808

Prelude

Allemande*

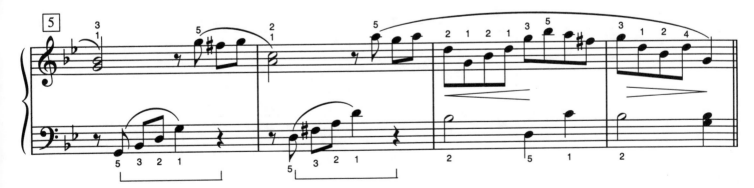

*A slow dance, generally placed at the beginning of a suite.

EL00194A

Courante*

Moderato

*A fast dance distinguished by many dotted rhythms.

Sarabande*

Largo

mp con espressione

*A slow, stately dance which is always in triple meter.

Gavotte*

Vivace

*A lively dance beginning on an upbeat, generally played after a sarabande.

Musette

Tranquillo

Gigue*

Allegro

*A fast, light dance (jig) generally used to end a suite.

MINUET IN G MINOR

from *The Notebook for Anna Magdalena Bach*

The original notebook of 1725 was a gift to Bach's wife, Anna Magdalena. Some of the compositions were intended for the educational purposes of the Bach children. Other keyboard works including The *Well Tempered Clavier Book 1* and the *Clavier Book for Wilhelm Friedemann Bach* were also written during this period of Bach's life.

BWV115

MINUET IN G MINOR

Unlike the vocal music and the chamber and orchestral works, Bach's output for keyboard instruments stretches from the very beginnings of his activities as a composer up to his last months. Especially however, during his Cöthen and Leipzig periods, Bach wrote many keyboard pieces for concert performance and for teaching.

BWV822

GAVOTTE

from *French suite No. 5 in G Major*

The "French Suites" were written in Cöthen when Bach was chapel master of Prince Leopold on Anhalf. He called them suites for the harpsichord. The title "French Suites" was given to them later, possibly due to their French dance-like character. Bach preferred 2/2 meter to portray the French gavotte as a light and sprightly ballroom dance. Here, the half notes are the unit of time rather than the quarter notes.

BWV816

(Allegro) (♩ = 80)

FRENCH SUITE No. 3
A condensed arrangement of the entire suite

Just as the name "English Suites" was probably chosen because of the influence of the Englishman Henry Purcell, Bach's "French Suites" show the charm and distinctive dance-like characteristics of Couperin's French style. As with the "English Suites," Bach composed six suites each with six pieces. During the baroque period, "Suite" was the musical term for a set of dance tunes linked together by a common key and common thematic material.

BWV814

Allemande*

*A slow dance, generally placed at the beginning of a suite.

Courante*

*A fast dance in ¾ time, to contrast with the Allemande.

Sarabande*

*A slow dance with strongly accentuated and majestic rhythm.

Minuet*

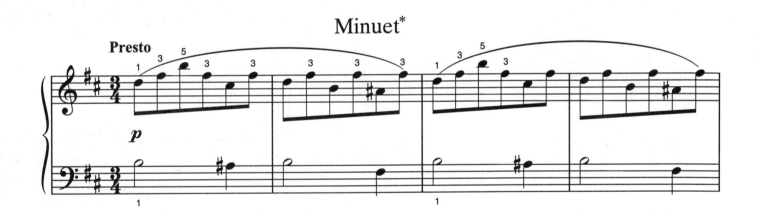

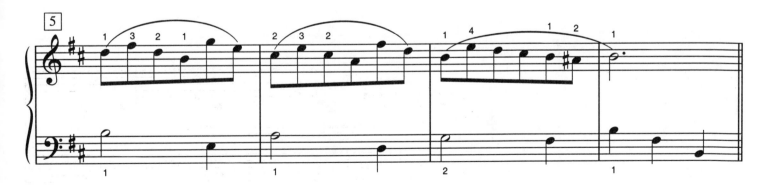

*A dance of French origin, not found in all suites.

Anglaise*

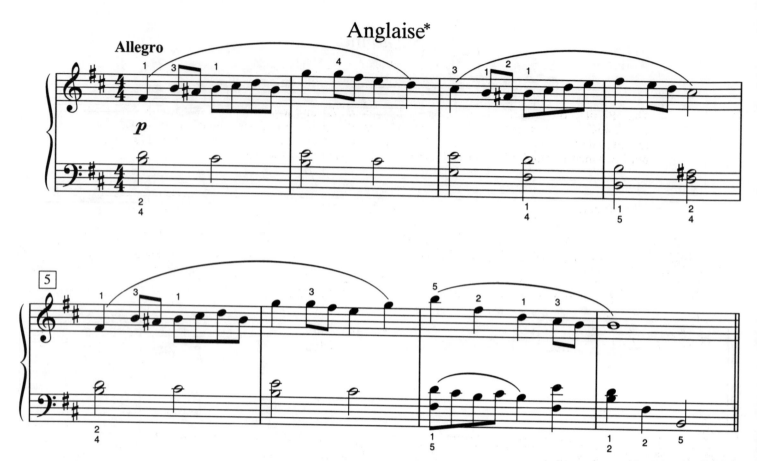

*An English country dance.

Gigue*

*A fast, light dance (jig) generally used to end a suite.

PARTITA No. 1
A condensed arrangement of the entire suite

This "Partita," the first of a set of six, was published in 1726 and was inscribed Opus. 1 indicating
that it was Bach's first printed work. "Partita" is another name used during the baroque period
for "Suite" or set of pieces. Originally the term referred to a group of dances played consecutively,
but Bach incorporated other musical forms as well as dance forms into his "Partitas."

BWV825

Minuet II

Gigue

PRELUDE IN D MINOR

In 1729, Bach took over the collegium musicum in Leipzig. The collegium had been founded by Telemann in 1704 and was a voluntary association of professional musicians and university students that gave regular weekly public concerts. Although nothing is known of the programs for these weekly concerts, it is generally acknowledged that Bach must have given performances of many of his Cöthen instrumental works.

BWV935

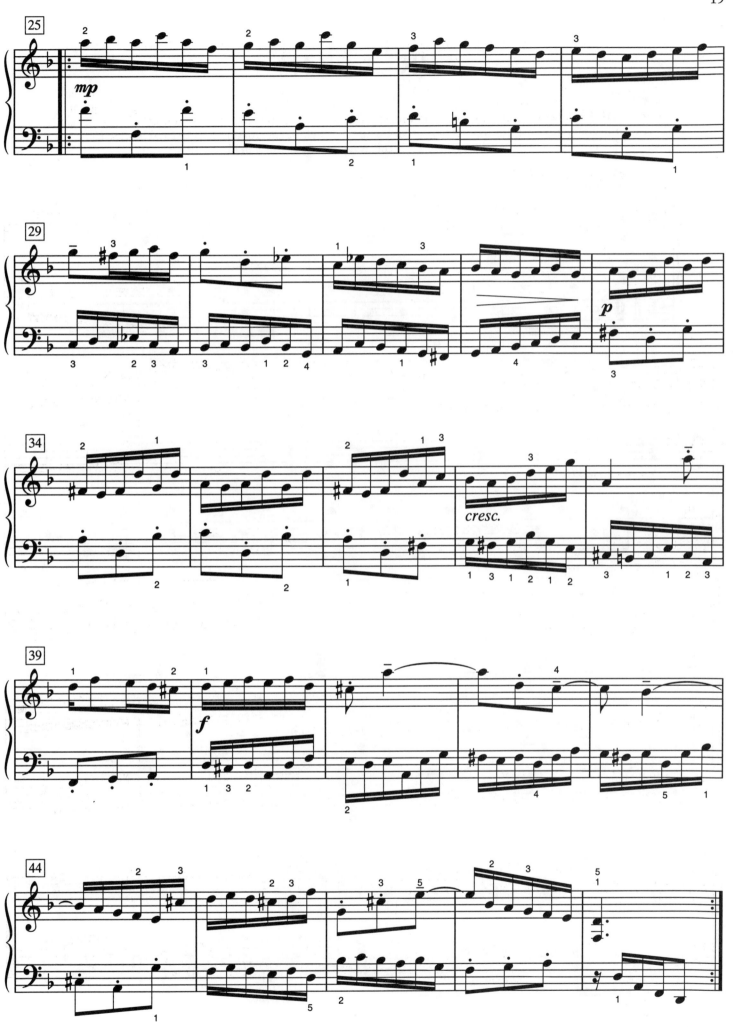

PRELUDE

The Bach Gesellschaft was a German society founded in 1850 for the purpose of publishing the complete works of Johann Sebastian Bach. The prelude included here is from "The Bach Society's Complete Works Volume IV." This is an excellent study in alternating hands.

ARIA IN D MINOR

from *The Notebook for Anna Magdalena Bach*

Two versions of this piece were included in the notebook. The melody line and
words appear in Anna Magdalena's own hand. J.S. Bach added the bass line later.

BWV515

PRELUDE No. 5
from *The Well Tempered Clavier*

Bach composed *The Well Tempered Clavier* at a time when efforts were being made to devise the system of tempered tuning still used on keyboard instruments today. Bach was especially interested in exploring the entire range of major and minor keys.

BWV850

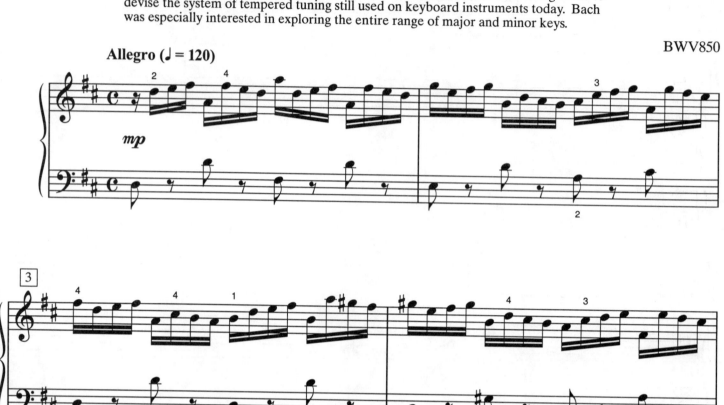

PRELUDE No. 15
from *The Well Tempered Clavier*

Bach wrote out the 24 preludes and fugues for *The Well Tempered Clavier*
in 1722. His pupils made a number of handwritten copies from the original
manuscript. This exuberant prelude is basically constructed from broken chords.

BWV860

*Bach indicated $\frac{24}{16}$ in the original edition.

EL00194A

John W. Schaum
(1905–1988)

Founder and director of the Schaum Music School in Milwaukee, Wisconsin, John W. Schaum is the composer of internationally famous piano teaching materials including more than 200 books and 450 sheet music pieces. He is author of the internationally acclaimed *Schaum Piano Course* published by Belwin-Mills Publishing Corporation/Warner Bros. Publications. During his extensive travels, Mr. Schaum presented hundreds of piano teacher workshops in all fifty states. He was president of the Wisconsin Music Teachers Association and soloist with the Milwaukee Philharmonic Orchestra.

Mr. Schaum received a master of music degree from Northwestern University, a bachelor of music degree from Marquette University, and a bachelor of music education degree from the University of Wisconsin-Milwaukee.

He remains an important influence in the lives of hundreds of thousands of piano students who have enjoyed and continue to play his music.